W9-AAW-312

Coyote is always
out there waiting,
and Coyote is
always hungry.

www.rourkepublishing.com

Editor: Frank Sloan

Pedro and The Coyote is based on the well-known rabbit and coyote folktales told throughout Mexico and Latin America. *Star Mountain and Other Legends of Mexico* by Camilla Campbell includes examples of these.

To Shahri, with love
S.S.

Library of Congress Cataloging-in-Publication Data

Sepehri, Sandy.
Pedro and the coyote : based on Mexican folktales / retold by Sandy Sepehri ; illustrated by Brian Demeter.
p. cm. -- (Latin American tales and myths)
ISBN 1-60044-149-1
1. Tales--Latin America. I. Demeter, Brian, ill. II. Title.
III. Series.
GR114.S43 2007
398.20972--dc22
2006014934

Printed in the USA

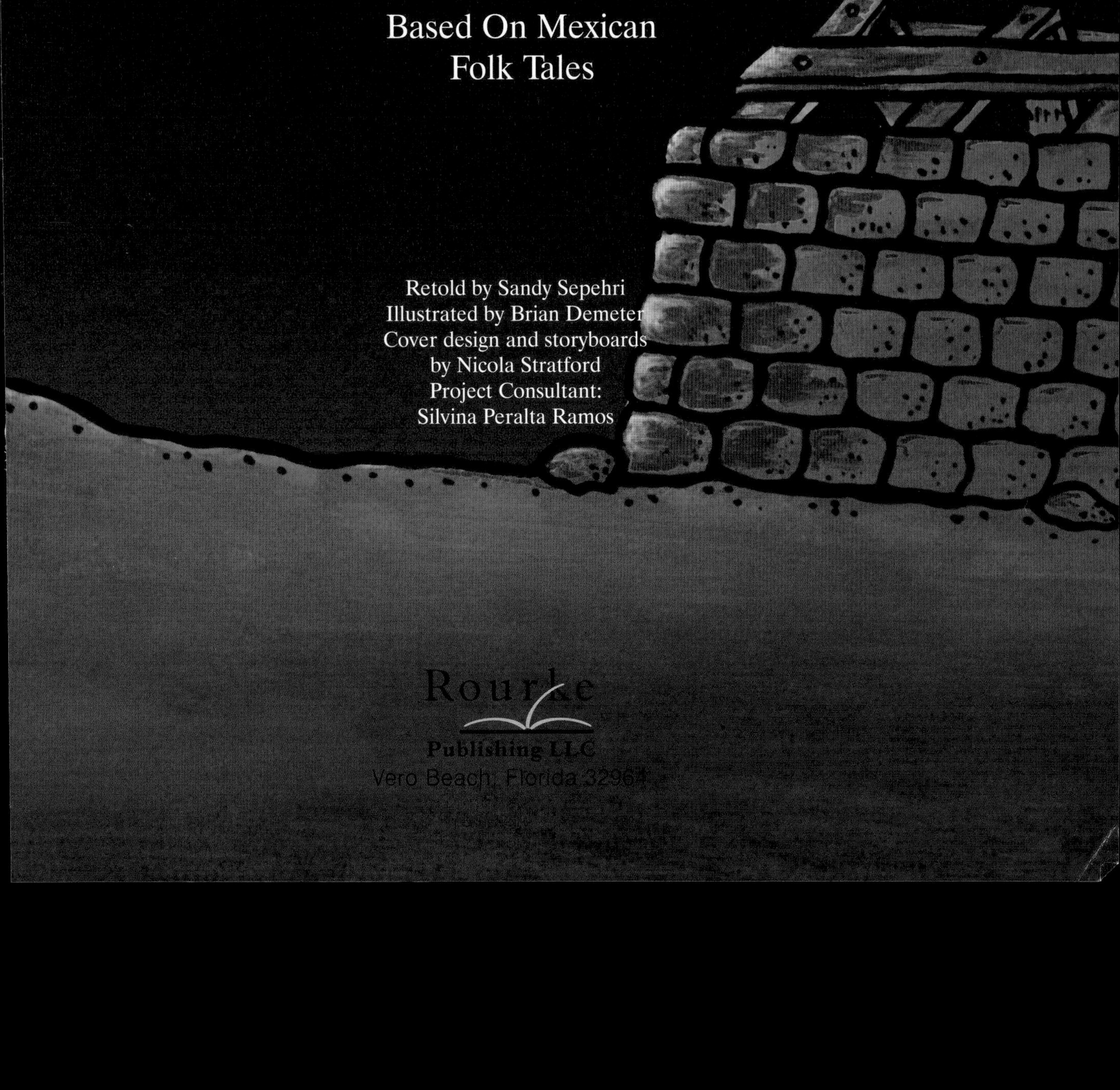

Based On Mexican
Folk Tales

Retold by Sandy Sepehri
Illustrated by Brian Demeter
Cover design and storyboards
by Nicola Stratford
Project Consultant:
Silvina Peralta Ramos

Rourke
Publishing LLC
Vero Beach, Florida 32964

In **Guanajuato**, Mexico, little Pedro was known as a good boy. Although he was only eight, he was a hard worker who helped his parents run their farm.

Pedro's **padre** had much to do with his crops. And his **madre** was busy with Maria, Pedro's **hermana**. There was always plenty of work for Pedro. And he loved the work.

The first thing he did each morning was to feed the animals. During the day he helped his padre shear the sheep, and he helped his madre milk the cows. And he took care of the chickens all by himself.

he chicken coop looked like a small house. It was made of clay bricks that Pedro and his padre had made themselves. The roof was open to the sky but the chickens could not fly out of their coop.

Pedro loved the chickens and had even named them. He would say, “**Buenos dias**,” Carlota, Caterina, Luisa, Teresa, Isabella, and Angelina.” Every morning he checked to see if they had laid eggs. If so, his madre used them to make **huevos rancheros** for his breakfast.

Those were perfect days. A day that was not perfect was when he had a visit from **Señor** Coyote.

Pedro's madre had always told him stories about fierce coyotes. Coyotes with blood-red eyes, razor-sharp teeth, and horns hidden behind their ears.

Because of these stories, Pedro would lie in his bed every night, tormented by nightmarish visions of coyotes.

One coyote Pedro had named Señor Coyote. This coyote would come down from his home in the mountains and sneak up on their farm, looking for a meal of fresh chicken. Pedro's padre would scare the coyote away by firing his pistol in the air.

But Señor Coyote kept returning until he found a small opening in the chicken coop. With his paw he pushed away some bricks, and made a small hole large enough for him to squeeze through.

Señor Coyote had to squirm and wriggle to get through the opening, but he was so skinny that he could just fit in the hole.

With a final wriggle, Señor Coyote slid into the chicken coop and saw the six chickens. He was very hungry, so he quietly stood in front of Angelina's roost. He flashed his eyes, and Angelina became so dizzy watching him that she fell off her roost and straight into Señor Coyote's mouth.

Señor Coyote helped himself to Caterina and Isabella in the same way! Then he decided to leave before the farmer awoke. He tried to leave the coop through the opening he had entered.

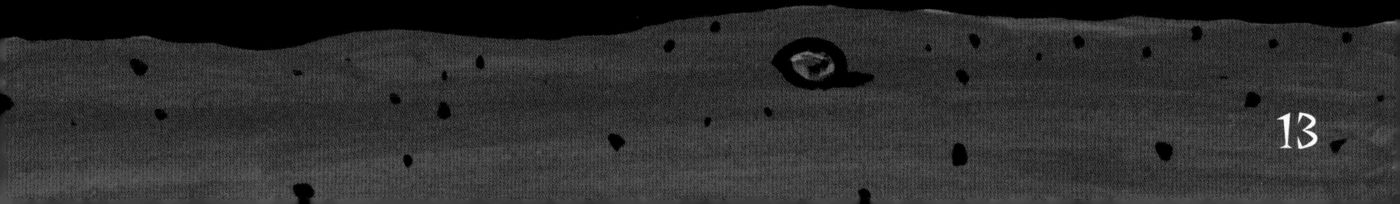

He slid his snout through the hole, and then his shoulders. But, when he got to his stomach, he got stuck! Unlike when he first entered the coop, his stomach was now packed with three fat chickens, and he simply would not fit through the hole. Hearing the sound of people stirring around in their house, Señor Coyote knew he had to come up with a plan to save himself – and quickly!

When Pedro entered the coop, through its door, he immediately noticed the three empty roosts. "**Papi**! Papi!" he called, for his padre. "Come quickly! Half of our chickens are gone!

Pedro's padre entered the coop. "Look, **hijo**," there's the thief. It looks as though he's had his last meal!"

Pedro looked in the corner and there was Señor Coyote, lying on his back. His legs stuck out straight and stiff, his mouth wide open.

"¡**Caramba**!" he cried, "he must have stuffed himself to death!"

Pedro tied a rope to Señor Coyote's back leg and dragged the animal away, far from the farm. Before he left the dead animal, Pedro looked at the dead coyote's legs sticking straight up in the air. He thought the creature looked more like an upside down table than a fierce coyote.

"You are not worthy to die with my three chickens in your stomach, Señor Coyote. And I was foolish enough to be afraid of you! It seems that your own greedy stomach defeated you!" Pedro turned and slowly began to walk home.

Señor Coyote listened as carefully as he could, waiting and waiting for Pedro to get far enough away from him, where he couldn't catch him, but not too far to miss seeing him jump up from the ground. "¡**Ay, muchacho**!" shouted Señor Coyote.

Pedro turned around and saw Señor Coyote standing tall, looking rested, and shouting "**Muchas gracias** for the meal! You cannot believe everything you see, **niño estúpido**!" Then the coyote started running home to the mountain, where Pedro would never find him.

Pedro was furious. He knew that Señor Coyote would return for the other three chickens. He quickly went to work patching the hole in the coop.

The next night, Pedro asked his parents if he could go fishing. He took his fishing pole to a quiet pond between his farm and where the coyote lived. He was sure Señor Coyote would see him there when he came back for more chicken!

And Pedro was right! Señor Coyote crept down from his home, with chicken on his mind! When he saw Pedro sitting calmly by the pond, he was very curious.

"Hey!" said Señor Coyote, "What keeps you on the edge of this pond, instead of snug in your bed, tonight?"

"That huge piece of cheese floating in the pond," Pedro answered. "I want to eat it, but I don't want to get my clothes wet, so I'm trying to pull it out with my fishing hook."

Then Pedro tried to look as if he was just getting a brilliant idea.

"I know," he shouted. "If you can think of a way to get the cheese from the water, I'll share it with you."

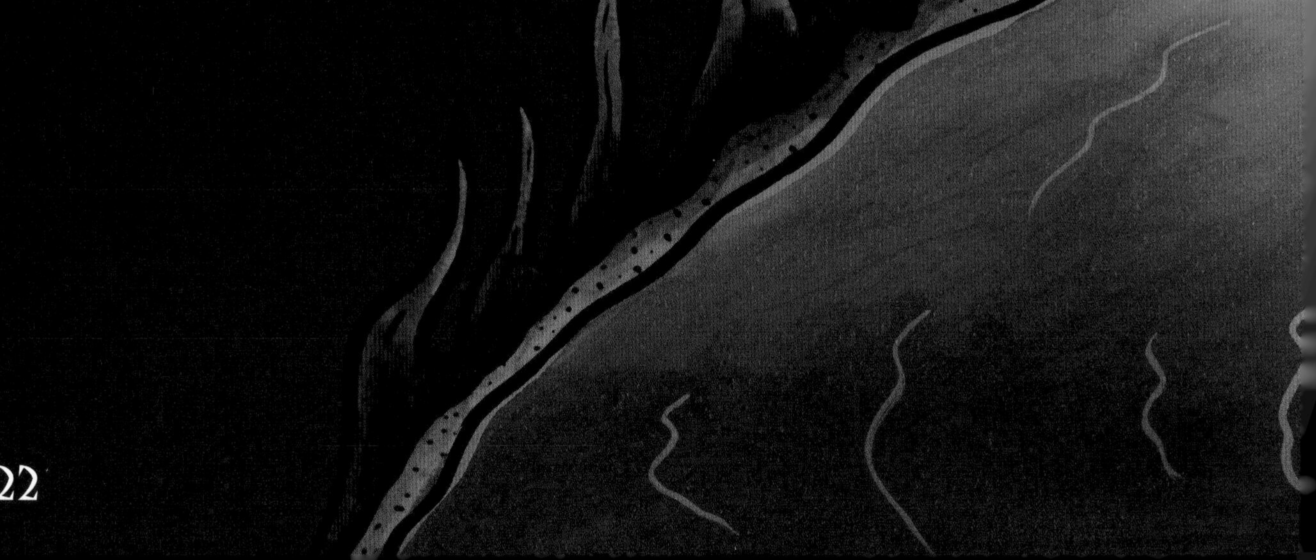

Señor Coyote had tasted cheese once before—and loved it. But he had never found any again until tonight. And what a large piece of cheese it was! Of course, he could think of a way to get it out of the water, but sharing it was not part of his plan.

Watch me," the coyote shouted as he jumped into the pond and quickly swam over to the giant piece of cheese. But he couldn't grab the cheese, and all he tasted was simply a mouthful of water. He kept getting more and more water, but no cheese.

"Where is the cheese, **amigo**?" Señor Coyote sputtered.

"Amigo?" Pedro scoffed. "Why do you call me estúpido when you are full with my chickens but not when you are full with the moon's reflection? You can look all night," Pedro continued, "but all you will find is the bottom of the pond!"

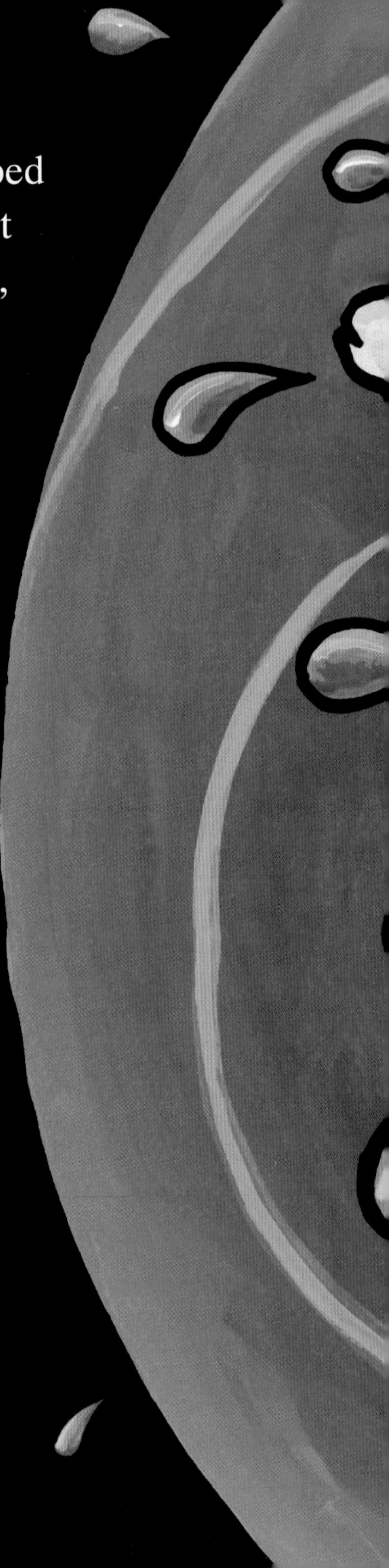

Señor Coyote looked up at the night sky and realized the trick that had been played on him. Knowing that his legs were too weary to carry him back to shore, he pleaded with Pedro to save him. “I promise I will never again steal from your farm.”

Not wishing to harm any creature, Pedro reached out and pulled the coyote back to land.

"That was a clever trick, amigo!" Señor Coyote said.

"**Sí**," answered Pedro. "When you look through eyes with cruelty and greed, you do not see things so clearly. I am not stupid. And there is no cheese in the pond!"

Pedro had made a fool of Señor Coyote. He was no longer a fearsome creature to Pedro. Wet and exhausted, he slunk back to his home, never to return.

Pedro spent the rest of the night fishing and returned home with his catch. His hermana was waiting for him with delicious huevos rancheros!

Glossary

amigo (am EE go) — friend
ay, muchacho (eye moo CHA choe) — hey, boy
buenos dias (bwey NOES DEE ahs) — good day
caramba (car RAHM bah) — oh, no!
Guanajuato (gwah nah HUA toe) — the capital of the Mexican state of the same name, known for its historical monuments and deposits of silver and gold discovered by Spaniards.
hermana (er MON ah) — sister
hijo (EE hoe) — son
huevos rancheros (way VOSE ran CHAIR ose) — ranch-style omelet
Madre (mod RAY) — mother
muchas gracias (moo CHAAS gras SEE ahs) — thanks very much
niño estúpido (neen YO stu pee DOE) — stupid child
Padre (pod RAY) — father
Papi (pa PEE) — Daddy
Señor (sin YOUR) — Mr.
Sí (SEE) — yes

About The Author

Sandy Sepehri lives with her husband, Shahram, and their three children in Florida. She has a bachelor's degree and writes freelance articles and children's stories.